Psalms for FATHERS

GOD'S GIFT
OF ENDLESS LOVE,
JOY, AND ENCOURAGEMENT

HONOR
BOOKS

Honor Books
Tulsa, Oklahoma

Psalms for Fathers
ISBN 1-56292-843-0

Copyright © 2001 by GRQ Ink, Inc.
1948 Green Hills Blvd.
Franklin, Tennessee 37067

Published by Honor Books
P. O. Box 55388
Tulsa, Oklahoma 74155

Developed by GRQ Ink, Inc.
Manuscript written by Andrew McLeod
Cover and text design by Whisner Design Group
Composition by Educational Publishing Concepts, Inc.

Your wife will be like a fruitful vine
within your house;
your sons will be like olive shoots
around your table.
Thus is the man blessed
who fears the Lord.

—⁂—

PSALM 128:3-4 NIV

God Loves a Father's Prayer

His delight is in the law of the LORD,
and on his law he meditates day and night.
He is like a tree planted by streams of water,
which yields its fruit in season and whose leaf does not wither.
Whatever he does prospers.

PSALM 1:2-3 NIV

—⟋⟋⟋—

*F*athers are great prayer-makers. One look at our children as they leave for school, play with their friends in the front yard, or

open birthday presents can bring a prayer to our lips. We pray constantly for their protection. We're proud of them and give thanks for them. We beg God to guide them as they grow. We ask God to help us be good fathers. God loves a father's prayers. We talk so much with God because our children are so wonderful. There's so much to say—we want our children to be held in the palm of God's hand.

God says much to us when we listen with our hearts. God tells us not to worry, but to have faith in God's goodness. God tells us that He loves our children even more than we do. God promises to work through us as we raise our children the best we can.

—⟋⟋⟋—

*W*e can pray to God today because God listens to our prayers.

I cried unto the LORD with my voice,
and he heard me out of his holy hill.

PSALM 3:4 KJV

―ᴟ―

In the morning, O LORD, You will hear my voice;
In the morning I will
order my prayer to You and eagerly watch.

PSALM 5:3 NASB

God Is Our Shield

You, O LORD, are a shield around me,
my glory, and the one who lifts up my head.

PSALM 3:3 NRSV

———

*F*athers have a special job—to protect our children so that they can grow up healthy and happy. We work hard to provide for their health and well-being. We make sure they have a good, safe home. We hold their hands when we cross the street. We help them learn how to take care of themselves, and we teach them what we know about life.

We also call on God to protect our children, to shield them with the brightness of His light, and to hide them in the shadow of His wings. Praying for God's protection is as important as making sure our kids have their seat belts fastened. God covers our children with His goodness and mercy. God journeys with them by day and watches over them by night.

God is our shield too. God watches over fathers and helps us to raise healthy, happy children. God's shield is very big—it covers our children and us as surely as a warm blanket on a cold winter's night.

———

*W*e can relax today knowing that God is our shield.

GOD's my island hideaway,
keeps danger far from the shore,
throws garlands of hosannas around my neck.
PSALM 32:7 THE MESSAGE

—⁓—

You bless righteous people, O LORD.
Like a large shield, you surround them with your favor.
PSALM 5:12 GOD'S WORD

Love Watches Over Us

*I sleep and wake up refreshed
because you, LORD, protect me.*

PSALM 3:5 CEV

———

*I*t's been another busy day. A full day at work. A soccer match after work. Later there was homework to supervise and bedtime stories to read. Through all the activity God's love watches over our kids and us dads.

Because God's love watches over us, we can go about the business of raising our children free from worry or anxiety. No matter how busy we are, God's love, like the air we breathe, sustains us. God's love wraps about us, like a favorite, well-worn sweatshirt. No matter what we do, we can count on the power of God's love watching over us to make everything all right. No matter where we go, the love of God follows us and gives us the strength we need to be good dads.

God's first words to us in the morning are *I love you*, and His last words to us at night are *I love you*. With love like that, we can do anything.

———

*T*he power of God's love is with us now.

I trust in your love.
My heart is happy because you
saved me.
PSALM 13:5 NCV

—✦—

The LORD is merciful, compassionate, patient,
and always ready to forgive.
PSALM 145:8 GOD'S WORD

Morning with God

I will sing of your might;
I will sing aloud of your steadfast love in the morning.
For you have been a fortress for me
and a refuge in the day of my distress.

PSALM 59:16 NRSV

———ɯ———

*M*ornings are not necessarily the most peaceful time of the day, especially on school days. We help get the kids out of bed and into clothes. Get a little breakfast into them and supervise teeth brushing. Then packed lunches are distributed. Finally, the kids are off to school as we leave for work.

Thank God for weekends! We can get up a little early on a Saturday before the whole house wakes up, make a cup of coffee, get comfortable on the couch, and have a good talk with God. Saturday mornings are a good time to ask God for what we need. We spend the rest of the week making sure our families have what they need. Now it's our turn. Quietly drinking coffee on the couch, we listen very carefully for our hearts to tell us what we need from God.

———ɯ———

*G*od listens carefully to hear what it is we want from Him.

O LORD, You have heard the desire of the humble;
You will strengthen their heart,
You will incline Your ear.
PSALM 10:17 NASB

Open up before GOD, keep nothing back;
he'll do whatever needs to be done.
PSALM 37:5 THE MESSAGE

The Wonder of God

Here I am, your invited guest—
it's incredible!
I enter your house; here I am,
prostrate in your inner sanctum.

PSALM 5:7 THE MESSAGE

—꣺꣺—

*E*very father has experienced the power of wonder. When we first saw our child, we were overwhelmed by wonder. When we first

held our child, the wonder and awe of this complete and perfect little human brought tears to our eyes as we looked at what God created.

Our children may be babies now or be teenagers or have families of their own. No matter what their age, we still experience the wonder of God. Whenever we look at our children, whether they're toddlers or grown-ups, we can still see God's handiwork in them. When we see how God is at work in their lives, we wonder at the goodness of God. It's not unlike the first time we held them in our arms, filled with wonder and joy to see what God created.

—꣺꣺—

*W*e can look at our children and know the wonder of God.

There will be an abundance of grain in the earth,
On the top of the mountains;
Its fruit shall wave like Lebanon;
And those of the city shall flourish like grass of the earth.

PSALM 72:16 NKJV

—⁓⁓—

From everlasting to everlasting,
the LORD'S mercy is on those who fear him.
His righteousness belongs
to their children and grandchildren.

PSALM 103:17 GOD'S WORD

A Reason to Rejoice

Let all who take refuge in You be glad,
Let them ever sing for joy;
And may You shelter them,
That those who love Your name may exult in You.

PSALM 5:11 NASB

A father whose frightened kids have ever invaded his bedroom on a dark and stormy night knows that his children look to him to keep them safe. Our children look to us to keep them safe from

scary things—thunder and lightning, monsters under the bed, and things that go bump in the night. We chase the monsters away and tell them there's nothing to be afraid of. We're dads. It's our job.

It's God's job to take care of fathers. We can turn to God anytime and be held in His arms. We can trust God to chase away the worries and concerns we naturally have for our children. We can listen in the quiet of the night to God telling us there's nothing to be afraid of. Our God loves us, cares for us, and protects us. What a reason to relax—and be glad.

---

*W*e can be glad because it's God's job to take care of us.

They will sing about what the LORD has done,
because the LORD 's glory is great.
Though the LORD is supreme
he takes care of those who are humble.
but he stays away from those who are proud.

PSALM 138:5-6 NCV

God's Children

Thou hast made him a little lower than the angels, and hast crowned him with glory and honour.

PSALM 8:5 KJV

—⁂—

*F*athers know that underneath the dirt and scruffiness of the play yard, and behind the usual acting out and unwillingness to clean their plates at dinner, our children seem like angels. When we peek in on our children and see them sound and peacefully asleep, we are convinced that our children do indeed have heavenly origins.

Our children are God's children—and so are we, their fathers. For we, too, are special creatures among all God's creation. God loves us. God has marked us as His own—He has crowned us with honor and glory. Like the angels in heaven, we shine with the love of God, our Father.

Now God has trusted us to raise and love and protect our children. We do so with a fierce father's love that shines brighter and stronger than the sun.

—⁂—

*W*e are God's children touched by His love.

You created my inmost being;
you knit me together in my mother's womb.
PSALM 139:13 NIV

~

The LORD is good;
his steadfast love endures forever,
and his faithfulness to all generations.
PSALM 100:5 NRSV

Bountiful Gifts

I will sing unto the Lord, because he hath dealt bountifully with me.

PSALM 13:6 KJV

—∿—

*L*ove is a father's greatest characteristic. The next greatest feature a father has is his ability to give. We are givers. Love is

behind all our gifts to our children. Of course, we give our children the basic necessities of life—food, clothing, shelter, education, and medical care. We also give limitless time and attention to help them grow up into good and loving adults. We make sure they learn about God and His ways, and about how much God loves them.

Just as we give good gifts to our children, God gives good gifts to us. God blesses us every day with the faith and courage to raise our children well. God touches us with His mercy and forgiveness, so that when we make mistakes, we can try again. God holds us in His love, which we give freely to our children.

—∿—

*G*od gives us gifts every moment today.

O LORD my God, you have done many miracles for us.
Your plans for us are too numerous to list.
If I tried to recite all your wonderful deeds,
I would never come to the end of them.

PSALM 40:5 NLT

A Father's Way

Lord, who may abide in Your tabernacle?
Who may dwell in Your holy hill?
He who walks uprightly,
And works righteousness,
And speaks the truth in his heart.

PSALM 15:1-2 NKJV

It's been said that "imitation is the highest form of flattery." Our children love to imitate us. Whether they are pretending to be daddies going to work or mimicking our conversation, children practice at being grown-ups by pretending they are their dads. Children naturally want to follow their fathers wherever they go, whatever they do, and whatever they say. Fathers show their children the way through life.

Part of our job is to show our children how to live so that they can follow us into happy adulthood. We speak truthfully to them and show them by our actions how much God loves them. This is a father's way—to "imitate" God's love. A father's way is God's way. When we speak and live God's love, our children naturally want to follow us and be like us. We raise our children to be merciful, wise, and loving grown-ups.

Today we travel a father's way and show our children how to follow God's way.

I am constantly aware of your unfailing love,
and I have lived according to your truth.

PSALM 26:3 NLT

—⁊⁊⁊—

LORD, you do everything for me.
LORD, your love continues forever.
You made us. Do not leave us.

PSALM 138:8 NCV

A Father's Identity

I said to the LORD,
"You are my Lord. Without you, I have nothing good."

PSALM 16:2 GOD'S WORD

—ᘯᘯ—

*F*athers are many things. We are lovers, caregivers, and providers. We are teachers, referees, and drivers. We are organizers, coaches, and champions. We enjoy being all those things because we like being dads.

We have a secret identity in addition to all those other things. We have been touched by God's goodness, chosen by God's love. We have been chosen to be God's special people—fathers. God has put a distinctive kind of love in our hearts. It is a love without end. That love marks us as God's chosen ones. We share that love with our children, whether we're being a garage-door handyman or a bicycle shade-tree mechanic or a homework supervisor. We know deep in our hearts how much God loves us. We know deep in our hearts that we are God's chosen people—we are fathers.

—ᘯᘯ—

*W*e are fathers, chosen by God's love.

Because you are my help,
I sing in the shadow of your wings.
My soul clings to you;
your right hand upholds me.
PSALM 63:7-8 NIV

Our Fathers before Us

The boundary lines have fallen for me in pleasant places;
surely I have a delightful inheritance.

PSALM 16:6 NIV

—⁂—

*F*atherhood is an ancient path we travel. Our fathers, our grandfathers, and our great-grandfathers before us have traveled the way of fatherhood. A father's wisdom is really a quiet knowledge stored up in our hearts. It is the knowledge that is gleaned from all our fathers gone before us. Fatherhood is a "delightful inheritance."

God gives us the heritage of fatherhood. We are the heirs of all the fatherly love and strength before us, and we are the stewards of all the fatherly love and strength that will come after us through our children. We are links in a vast chain of God's making, passing on that which is good and loving and true from father to child. As fathers we can be proud and humble at the same time for all we've inherited. We can be grateful to all our male ancestors—our fathers, who have handed us the torch of sacred fatherhood.

—⁂—

*W*e stand as a link in a long chain of fatherly love, blessed and held together by God.

A posterity shall serve Him.
It will be recounted of the LORD to the next generation,
They will come and declare His righteousness
to a people who will be born,
That He has done this.
PSALM 22:30-31 NKJV

—m—

Your kingdom will never end, and you will rule forever.
Our LORD, you keep your word and do everything you say.
PSALM 145:13 CEV

Fatherhood's Solid Foundation

I have set the LORD always before me;
Because He is at my right hand
I shall not be moved.

PSALM 16:8 NKJV

———⟫⟫———

*I*f we pick up any family magazine today, we can find countless guides to help us be better fathers. Our world will always be filled with teachers and leaders of various child-rearing techniques and fads. As helpful as some of these guides may be, we can always turn to a more solid foundation.

Our God is our foundation. God is our ultimate guide in all things—especially the care of our children. God is big enough and strong enough to help us in all we ask and in all we seek to do. No fad or force on the planet can move us, because God walks with us at our right side every moment of every day. We can turn to God and open our hearts, confident in God's mercy and love. We can turn to God and place our children in His gentle, loving hands.

———⟫⟫———

*O*ur solid foundation is God, who holds
us in the palm of His hand.

May He send you help from the sanctuary
And support you from Zion!

PSALM 20:2 NASB

——〰——

He is the one who made heaven and earth,
the sea, and everything in them.
He is the one who keeps every promise forever.

PSALM 146:6 NLT

Enjoying God

You have made known to me the path of life;
You will fill me with joy in your presence,
With eternal pleasures at your right hand.

PSALM 16:11 NIV

———m———

A lot of times being a father is fun. When we play with our children, it's almost like we get to be kids again. We get invited to Scout camp. We get to ride bikes and build forts out of blankets. Sometimes we get to go to Disneyland.

Play is also important to a father's walk with God. God enjoys us—and God wants to be enjoyed by us. God wants us to take pleasure in Him. That means we can have fun with God. We don't have to be serious all the time—we can let God into our playtime with our kids; we can lie in a hammock and daydream with God; we can take a long walk with God and not talk about anything much at all. Our relationship with God is to be enjoyed. Today, do something with God just for the fun of it.

———m———

*T*oday there's time to enjoy God.

Sing for joy to God our strength;
shout aloud to the God of Jacob!
Begin the music, strike the tambourine,
play the melodious harp and lyre.
Sound the ram's horn at the New Moon,
and when the moon is full, on the day of our Feast.
PSALM 81:1-3 NIV

—m—

O LORD my God, I will give thanks to you forever.
PSALM 30:12 NRSV

A Father's Prayer

I call upon you, for you will answer me, O God;
incline your ear to me, hear my words.

PSALM 17:6 NRSV

*F*athers spend a lot of time listening. When our children are young, we listen to their endless questions about how the world works and why it works the way it does. When our children are  teenagers we listen to them tell us all about school and their new boyfriends or about how much they need a car. When our children marry and have children of their own, we love to listen to stories about our grandchildren.

God spends a lot of time listening to fathers. God listens to us tell Him how proud we are of our children. God listens to us when we ask for strength and help to be the best fathers we can be. God listens to us as we place our children in His care. God loves to listen to a father's prayers. Know that whenever we call on God, He listens to every word we say.

*G*od loves to listen to a father's prayers.

Enjoy serving the LORD,
and he will give you what you want.
PSALM 37:4 NCV

—⁂—

I hope in You, O LORD;
You will answer, O LORD my God.
PSALM 38:15 NASB

The Love of God

"I love You, O Lord, my strength."
The Lord is my rock and my fortress and my deliverer,
My God, my rock, in whom I take refuge;
My shield and the horn of my salvation, my stronghold.

PSALM 18:1-2 NASB

—⟋⟋⟍—

*E*verything about fatherhood can be summed up in one word—
love. Everything we do, everything we say, and every ounce of our

being is motivated by love. Our giving, our patience, our compassion, our strength, our understanding, and our hope— all of fatherhood's qualities are rooted in the love we have for our children.

Everything about God can also be summed up in one word—*love.* As hard as it is to imagine, God's love for us is deeper, more powerful, and more all-knowing than even a father's love. There is nothing we can do or think or say that can keep God from loving us. God follows us into the secret places of our hearts to tell us how much He loves us. We are God's children—and God loves us fiercely, deeply, and eternally.

—⟋⟋⟍—

*G*od's love for us is so great that nothing in heaven
or on earth can separate us from Him.

Pour out your unfailing love on those who love you;
give justice to those with honest hearts.

A Father's Night-light

Thou wilt light my candle: the L<small>ORD</small> my God will enlighten my darkness.

P<small>SALM</small> 18:28 <small>KJV</small>

—⟋⟍—

"If you turn off the lights, it'll be dark and the monsters in the closet will come out and get me!" What father hasn't heard, at some time or other, a child's reason like this one for keeping a light on at bedtime? So we compromise—we turn out the main light in the room, but we turn on a night-light to keep the monsters away.

Our faith in God is a father's "night-light." Unfortunately, we can't see into our children's futures—the way is dark and hidden from view. We can hope that our children's futures will be bright, however, because we believe God loves them and holds them in the palm of His hand. It's okay that we can't see into our children's future—because we know that God, who is our lamp, is there ahead of us lighting the way.

—⟋⟍—

God makes our children's futures bright.

The statutes of the LORD are right, rejoicing the heart;
The commandment of the LORD is pure, enlightening the eyes.

PSALM 19:8 NKJV

———ɯ———

You will help me, Lord God, and keep me from falling.

PSALM 54:4 CEV

God's Glory

The heavens declare the glory of God;
the skies proclaim the work of his hands.

PSALM 19:1 NIV

"Twinkle, twinkle little star" is one of the first tunes a child learns to sing. Children seem naturally drawn to the stars; they look up at the heavens, their imaginations winging through time and space. Our children are constantly pointing us to the glory of God.

We have a lot to teach our children, but our children have a lot to teach us as well. Maybe children can show us the glory of God in the heavens because they've so recently come from God. Not yet set in adult ways, their minds are still fresh and full of God's glory. On a warm summer's evening, we can let our children take us by the hand and lead us out to the backyard. There we can look up at the soft night sky, full of stars, the handiwork of God—and we can let the children tell us stories of what they see there.

The glory of God shines over us. All we have to do is look up.

The glory of the LORD shall endure for ever:
the LORD shall rejoice in his works.
PSALM 104:31 KJV

—⁓—

Who can forget the wonders he performs?
How gracious and merciful is our LORD!
He gives food to those who trust him;
he always remembers his covenant.
PSALM 111:4-5 NLT

A Father's Powerful Words

Let the words of my mouth and the meditation of my heart
Be acceptable in Your sight, O Lord, my rock and my Redeemer.

PSALM 19:14 NASB

———

A father's words are very powerful. Our words instruct our children, telling them right from wrong. Our words communicate our pride and caring. Our words correct our children when they

misbehave. A father's words have a tremendous impact on the shape of our children's lives and spirits.

Our words are powerful in another way. Our words have a tremendous impact on God. God listens carefully to what we have to say—and He is influenced by what we say. So we must choose our words carefully. Our prayers to God should always be said with love and honor—and always end in gratitude for the blessings of this life. We want our words to be pleasing and acceptable to God, who loves us and wants to give us His best.

———

*M*ay the words of our mouths be acceptable to God today.

I entreated Your favor
with my whole heart;
Be merciful to me
according to Your word.
PSALM 119:58 NKJV

—⚬—

Praise the LORD!
I will thank the LORD with all my heart
as I meet with his godly people.
PSALM 111:1 NLT

Our Heart's Desire

*May he give you the desire of your heart
and make all your plans succeed.*

PSALM 20:4 NIV

—⚜—

A father wants the best of everything for his children. We
naturally want our kids to have the best homes, the best schools,
and the best jobs. We want them to have the brightest futures. We
want them to be successful in work and in life. So far as it is within
our power, we want to give them the desires of their hearts.

We are God's children. God naturally
wants us to have the very best of
everything life has to offer. Even
more, God longs to give us our
deepest desires. What do our
hearts desire the most? If we
look long and hard and deeply
into the secret places of our
hearts, we find this simple
desire—we want God. We want
our children to want God more than
anything in the world. It is that desire
above all others that God is delighted to
grant.

—⚜—

*M*ay God grant all your desires and fulfill all your plans.

I truly believe
I will live to see the LORD's goodness.
PSALM 27:13 NCV

As for me, I trust in You, O LORD, I say, "You are my God."
PSALM 31:14 NASB

The Great Shepherd

The LORD is my shepherd; I shall not want.
He makes me to lie down in green pastures;
He leads me beside the still waters.

PSALM 23:1-2 KJV

A father's job, of course, is to take care of his children. So we spend a lot of our time as caregivers. It's a rewarding job, but it can also be tiring. Fathers need to be taken care of, too, if we're to continue to give the best of ourselves.

God, the Great Shepherd, is a father's caregiver. The Great Shepherd takes care of us by giving us direction in our lives. He walks beside us every day, leading and guiding us in the way we should go. He provides r us. He gives us what we need spiritually. He leads us to still ters and green pastures to restore our souls.

that the Great Shepherd needs from us is a willingness to fo Iim. We only need to trust Him, one step at a time, to take care every moment of every day.

To follow God with open and willing hearts.

I look up to the hills,
but where does my help come from?
My help comes from the LORD,
who made heaven and earth.
He will not let you be defeated.
He who guards you never sleeps.

PSALM 121:1-3 NCV

—m—

I am like an olive tree,
thriving in the house of God.
I trust in God's unfailing love
forever and ever.

PSALM 52:8 NLT

God's Hands

The earth and everything on it belong to the Lord.
The world and its people belong to him.

PSALM 24:1 CEV

—⧓—

*T*he children sing "He's got the whole world in His hands" in Sunday school. Straight from the mouths of babes comes this simple truth—God, the Creator of this planet and all the stars above, is in control. God is in control of the great universe—and God is in control of our small, but important, lives.

For fathers this truth comes as a great relief. What freedom! Because God's got the whole world in His hands, we can let God do His job and we are free to do our job. We don't have to be in total control all the time—we can relax knowing that our lives and the lives of our children are in God's capable hands. Since we don't have to be in total control, all fathers have to do is be responsible and do the best we can—we can leave the rest to God.

—⧓—

*W*e can relax today because
God's got the whole world in His hands.

Yes, the LORD pours down his blessings.
Our land will yield its bountiful crops.
PSALM 85:12 NLT

O, Lord, you have been our refuge throughout every generation.
Before the mountains were born, before you gave birth to the earth
and the world, you were God.
You are God from everlasting to everlasting.
PSALM 90:1-2 GOD'S WORD

God, Our Teacher

Show me your ways, O Lord,
teach me your paths;
guide me in your truth and teach me,
for you are God my Savior,
and my hope is in you all day long.

PSALM 25:4-5 NIV

———⁓———

We teach our children. We do much more than help them with their homework. Fathers teach what kids can't get out of a

textbook or a classroom—we teach our children right from wrong, and show them how to love God, others, and themselves. Where do fathers go to get this knowledge?

We turn to God and His words in the Bible. We humbly ask God to instruct our hearts in His way and truth. From God and the Bible we learn right from wrong, and we learn how to love God, others, and ourselves. We pass that knowledge on to our children. When we teach the way of God, we give them a gift more valuable than mere book knowledge—we give them the gift of how to live a happy life at peace with God.

———⁓———

God will teach us His way and truth today.

He leads humble people to do what is right,
and he teaches them his way.
Every path of the LORD is one of mercy and truth
for those who cling to his promise and written instructions.
PSALM 25:9-10 GOD'S WORD

God's House

—m—

Our homes are important to us. It's the place where we can be ourselves. It's the place we feel safest, happiest, and most relaxed. As fathers, we enjoy taking care of our homes—improving them and repairing them. After all, it's where we raise our children. There's no place like home.

We have another home too. God's home is also our home and our children's home. We go to God's house whenever we go to church, and yet God's home is bigger than any church. God's home is anywhere God lives. God's home is as big as heaven and as small as the secret, inner room in our hearts. We love the house in which God dwells—whether it's our local church or the depths of our own hearts. We can go home to visit God and enjoy God's glory anytime we like. God's house is around us, above us, and inside us.

—m—

We can be at home with God anytime we like.

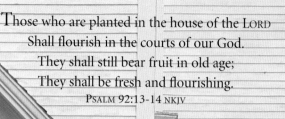

Those who are planted in the house of the LORD
Shall flourish in the courts of our God.
They shall still bear fruit in old age;
They shall be fresh and flourishing.
PSALM 92:13-14 NKJV

God's Peace

The LORD *is my light and my salvation; whom shall I fear? the* LORD *is the strength of my life; of whom shall I be afraid?*

PSALM 27:1-2 KJV

Family, friends, and media tell us how challenging fatherhood can be. "Just wait till they're teenagers." "Paying for college takes a lot of sacrifices." "Your life just isn't your own until they graduate." As if we didn't know. So what? We know that being a father is the toughest job we'll ever love—challenges included.

With God on our side we can do anything. There is nothing and no one to be afraid of. With God in our corner as we raise and love our children, certainly no challenge is too complicated, no obstacle is insurmountable, and no problem is insoluble. God is the strength of our lives and the lives of our children. Sure, being a father can be a tough job—but it's also an infinitely joyful one when we trust God to work all things for good.

God is our light and our salvation.
With God all things are possible.

I will listen
to what God the LORD will say;
he promises peace to his people,
his saints—
but let them not return to folly.
PSALM 85:8 NIV

—m—

He alone is my rock and my savior—
my stronghold.
I cannot be severely shaken.
PSALM 62:2 GOD'S WORD

God Is Good

Give thanks to the LORD because he is good.
His love continues forever.

PSALM 136:1 NCV

—◠◠—

*I*t's all good. We watch our children grow and learn and love and laugh. We enjoy fatherhood with all of its blessings, rewards, and challenges. We wouldn't change places with anyone else in the world. Being a father is all good.

The source of all goodness, of course, is God. God can't wait to pour His goodness on us— every moment of every day. We don't have to wait to get to heaven to experience how good God is. Any time we teach them how to ride a bike, help them with their homework, or watch them play in the backyard, we enjoy the goodness of God. Every time we hand out an allowance, hold a little hand to cross the street, or wave good-bye as they go off to summer camp, we touch God's goodness.

We are fathers. We are blessed. We have seen the goodness of the Lord in the land of the living.

—◠◠—

*W*e believe that we shall see the goodness of the Lord today.

Our LORD, everything you do is kind and thoughtful,
and you are near to everyone whose prayers are sincere.

PSALM 145:17-18 CEV

—⁂—

I will praise you forever for what you have done;
in your name I will hope, for your name is good.
I will praise you in the presence of your saints.

PSALM 52:9 NIV

The Power of Thanks

Sing praises to the LORD, O you his faithful ones,
and give thanks to his holy name.

PSALM 30:4 NRSV

———

"Thanks, Dad," she says after you've talked with her late into the night about her first prom. "Thanks, Dad," he says, hugging you, his college diploma gripped in his right hand. We don't do it for the thanks, of course. We do it out of love. We'd give them the whole world, if we could, for love alone. Hearing a thank-you is very nice, however. Like icing on a cake.

Imagine how God feels when we give Him a thank-You. Our thanks go right to God's heart. It's not just the big things in life we're grateful for. The smaller the blessing, the more powerful is our thanks to God who blesses us. We take nothing in our world for granted, for all good gifts come from God. God doesn't do it for the thanks, of course. Even though He does it out of love, He loves to hear His children give Him a thank-You.

———

Today we give a thank-You to God
for our world and all that is in it.

Be thankful and praise the Lord
as you enter his temple.
Psalm 100:4 CEV

—⁓—

Let everyone give thanks to you, O God.
Let everyone give thanks to you.
Psalm 67:3 GOD'S WORD

In God's Hand

Into your hands I commit my spirit;
redeem me, O LORD, the God of truth.

PSALM 31:5 NIV

—⟋⟍—

*J*ust getting out the door any weekday morning can be a challenge. Help get the kids up, supervise breakfast, and see that they're dressed. Drop them off at the bus stop or school. Then it's off to work and another busy day. With all that dads have to do in

the morning, it's easy to forget God. As we herd everybody out the door, we can pray a simple prayer to help us remember who's really driving this bus:

"Into Your hands I commit my spirit."

It says to God that He is in control of our life—not us. It says to God that we want to be with Him every moment of every day no matter how crazy today gets. It says to God that no matter what happens today, He brings goodness to all who love Him. It says to God that we love Him. Is there any better way for busy fathers to begin the day?

—⟋⟍—

O God, hear this simple prayer—
Into Your hands I commit my spirit.

I follow close behind you;
your strong right hand holds me securely.
PSALM 63:8 NLT

—m—

Through Thy righteousness, deliver me and set me free;
incline Thine ear to me and save me.
PSALM 71:2 MLB

The Joy of Forgiveness

Count yourself lucky, how happy you must be—
you get a fresh start,
your slate's wiped clean.

PSALM 32:1 THE MESSAGE

Sometimes we make mistakes. Sometimes we act without thinking. Sometimes we don't do our best even though our hearts are in the right place. Our intentions are full of love.

Thank God fathers can go to God for forgiveness! Forgiveness springs from deep love. When we ask God's forgiveness, God looks into our hearts and sees the love that's there. God forgives us. The joy of forgiveness is the ability to start over again. The joy of forgiveness is to try to love deeper and better than before. The joy of forgiveness is being able to forgive our children and families as God forgives us. The joy of forgiveness is freedom from being stuck in the past so we can try to love again.

The joy of God's forgiveness is available to us any time, day or night. Our God waits with open arms for us to experience the joy of forgiveness.

We can ask God's forgiveness any time we need to.

I come to you, LORD, for protection.
Don't let me be ashamed.
Do as you have promised and rescue me.
PSALM 31:1 CEV

—⁓—

As far as the east is from the west—
that is how far he has removed our rebellious acts from himself.
PSALM 103:12 GOD'S WORD

A Father's Blessing

—⁂—

*A*ll of us have experienced God's blessing. Of all the blessings of this life, none is greater than our children. Our children are God's blessings on us, God's love for us in flesh and blood.

God has greatly blessed us. How can we bless God? What could God possibly want or need from us? God wants to know that we love Him. Blessing God goes beyond thanking God— blessing God is saying we love Him, which is not always easy for men to do. Our blessings and praise of God put legs on our love for God—our words go straight to God's ears and into God's heart. Because we are fathers and are profoundly blessed by God with our children, we naturally return God's blessing by praising God in our hearts.

—⁂—

*W*e will bless the Lord all day long;
His praise will always be in our mouths.

We will celebrate and praise you, Lord!
You are good to us, and your love never fails.
PSALM 106:1 CEV

—⁂—

Hallelujah!
Praise the name of GOD,
praise the works of GOD.
All you priests on duty in GOD 's temple,
serving in the sacred halls of our God,
Shout "Hallelujah!" because GOD 's so good,
sing anthems to his beautiful name.
PSALM 135:1-3 THE MESSAGE

God's Faithfulness

God's love is meteoric,
his loyalty astronomic,
His purpose titanic,
his verdicts oceanic.

PSALM 36:5 THE MESSAGE

—⚬—

We know that God's greatest gift is faithfulness. We know that no matter what our children do (or don't do), we could never leave them. Because we are fathers, we stand with and by our children come what may. Even when our children grow up and have

families of their own, we never stop being their father. Fathers are faithful to their children throughout their lives.

No matter what we do (or don't do), God will never leave us. He is always faithful. God walks with us when times are good and sustains us when times are tough. God holds each of us in the palm of His hand regardless of how good we are. His love for us is so deep and wide that He journeys beside us, guiding us through thick and thin. God loves us fiercely with a father's kind of love. God's faithfulness will never let us go.

—⚬—

God's faithfulness toward us is as vast
as the heavens and as deep as the sea.

How excellent is thy lovingkindness, O God! therefore the children of
men put their trust under the shadow of thy wings.

PSALM 36:7 KJV

Let them give thanks to the LORD for his unfailing love
And his wonderful deeds for men,
For he satisfies the thirsty
and feeds the hungry with good things.

PSALM 107:8-9 NIV

Teach Your Children

I have been young, and now am old;
Yet I have not seen the righteous forsaken,
Nor his descendants begging bread.
He is ever merciful, and lends;
And his descendants are blessed.

PSALM 37:25-26 NKJV

———✺———

*F*athers are naturally generous people. We're good at giving. One of the most valuable gifts a father can give his child is a generous and open spirit. From that generous spirit a child can develop into a secure and confident adult who is able to give to others.

God wants us to teach our children about generosity. He assures us that when we give liberally our children become blessings. He returns generosity to us a hundredfold as our children put into practice what they learn from us—to give of themselves, their resources, their love, and their time unconditionally and without fear. We watch our children grow into generous adults who will one day teach their children the quiet spiritual reward of generosity.

———✺———

*G*od wants us to teach our children to give generously today.

I will instruct you and train you in the way you shall go;
I will counsel you with My eye on you.

PSALM 32:8 MLB

Waiting for God

Rest in the LORD and wait patiently for Him;
Do not fret because of him who prospers in his way,
Because of the man who carries out wicked schemes.

PSALM 37:7 NASB

———〜〜〜———

*F*athers know a lot about patience. Our children teach us. We must be patient when our children are learning how to do things for themselves, whether it's learning to tie their shoes or finishing a complicated set of math problems on a school night. We want them to hurry up. Patience tells us that we've got to let them learn at their own speed, if they are to learn well.

There's another kind of patience that fathers know about too. God teaches us. There are no hard and fast rules to being a good father. God wants us to learn as we go at our own speed. Sometimes we'd like to be like other fathers in the office or neighborhood, who seem to have it all together. God isn't finished with us yet. We must patiently wait for God to help us become good fathers day by day.

———〜〜〜———

*H*ave patience. God isn't finished with us yet.

Be strong, all who wait with hope for the LORD,
and let your heart be courageous.
PSALM 31:24 GOD'S WORD

—⟐—

Let your blessings reach me, O LORD.
Save me as you promised.
PSALM 119:41 GOD'S WORD

God's Law in a Father's Heart

I delight to do your will, O my God;
your law is within my heart.

PSALM 40:8 NRSV

———∞———

$\mathcal{I}$t takes a lot of physical energy to be a father these days. Just keeping up with our children can be a full-time job—except that we already have full-time jobs. It also takes a lot of spiritual and emotional energy to be a good father—because we give our hearts to our kids every day.

God renews our hearts, gives us the emotional and spiritual strength we need so we can be there for our children one hundred percent. When we keep God's law, God's Word, in our hearts, we find the energy we need for fatherhood. Reading the Bible and remembering favorite verses is a great spiritual boost after a demanding day at work. Keeping and meditating on God's law in our hearts gives us a peaceful spirit—a spirit that can help us manage anything.

———∞———

$\mathcal{W}$e have the energy we need for today because we keep God's law in our hearts.

The law of the LORD is perfect, converting the soul: the testimony of
the LORD is sure, making wise the simple.

PSALM 19:7 KJV

He counts the stars
and names each one.
Our LORD is great and very powerful.
There is no limit to what he knows.

PSALM 147:4-5 NCV

Praise Worthy

Then let me go to the altar of God, to God my highest joy,
and I will give thanks to you on the lyre, O God, my God.

PSALM 43:4 GOD'S WORD

—⁓—

*F*ather's Day is fun. A lot of what fathers do is taken for granted by our children. On Father's Day we get praise—we're showered with gifts, we're taken out for a meal, or the kids do our chores for us. Our churches recognize and honor us on Father's Day. It's a kick.

It's easy sometimes to take all God does for us for granted. The Bible tells us that God is worthy of praise. The next time we have a little time for ourselves, we might try this—proclaim God's Day. Keep a couple of favorite Bible verses at the top of your mind. Dedicate an exercise session to God. Make a list of blessings and thank God for each one. Let God's Day be a day remembering and praising God.

—⁓—

*T*oday is God's Day. Today we remember
God's work in our lives.

My praise shall be
of thee in the great
congregation:
I will pay my vows before
them that fear him.
PSALM 22:25 KJV

~m~

The LORD reigns,
let the earth be glad;
let the distant shores
rejoice.
PSALM 97:1 NIV

Simple Joy

O clap your hands, all peoples;
Shout to God with the voice of joy.

PSALM 47:1 NASB

———

*T*hink for a minute about the simple joys of fatherhood. Baby pulls herself up using the sofa and takes her first steps toward you across the carpet. She floats down the staircase in her first prom dress. Proudly, she accepts her college diploma from the dean. Looking tired, but blissful, in a hospital room she adjusts the

blanket that holds her own baby—the first grandchild. Nothing—no other experience, no amount of money—can compare to the simple joys and pride our children bring us.

Watching our children grow up, we are truly thankful. We are full of praise to our Creator, who makes all of these moments of joy and pride possible. It's enough to make us want to clap our

hands. God, looking down from heaven on our simple joy, rejoices with us—He claps and sings, and all the angels in heaven join in joy.

———

*G*o ahead—shout for joy. God touches our lives.

Great is the LORD and greatly to be praised
in the city of our God!
His holy mountain, beautiful in elevation,
is the joy of all the earth,
Mount Zion, in the far north,
the city of the great King.

PSALM 48:1-2 NRSV

Fathers Know

My mouth shall speak wisdom,
And the meditation of my heart shall give understanding.

PSALM 49:3 NKJV

—◊—

*I*t's common for many first-time fathers to fear that they won't know what do or how to help their wives care for their children. Some new fathers spend anxious months reading up on parenting. They grill friends with children about what to do; they tell their own fathers that maybe they're not quite ready for fatherhood. One day fatherhood comes, though, and a "father's instinct" kicks in, along with pride, and the new father just knows it's all going to be all right.

So it is in the life of faith. We don't need to know all the answers beforehand. We need only meditate in our hearts on the love of God day by day. God will give us the understanding and the knowledge we need to journey with Him. The understanding that God gives is like a father's instinct—we'll know what to do, and it'll be all right.

—◊—

*A*s we meditate on God's love in our hearts,
we'll know what God wants from us.

I will cry to the God of heaven
who does such wonders for me.
PSALM 57:2 TLB

I remember my song in the night
and reflect on it.
PSALM 77:6 GOD'S WORD

Trusting God

Nevertheless I am continually with you; you hold my right hand.

PSALM 73:23 NRSV

———※———

*W*e've all held the hand of our small children while crossing a busy street. Hand firmly in ours, the child carefully steps off the curb and follows at our side. The child is oblivious to the traffic, content to go where we lead, completely trusting without a thought or understanding of the danger involved in crossing any street.

God desires that same kind of trust from us. God promises to hold our hand no matter what. With our hand firmly in His, God asks that we trust Him, that we follow Him no matter where He leads us. We don't worry or fret. We know God's right hand holds our frail human hand. We follow at His side without a care in the world, knowing only that God's love has hold of us and our children.

———※———

*W*e can walk confidently through the day
because God holds our hands.

I will sing of the Lord's great love forever;
with my mouth I will make your faithfulness
known through all generations.
I will declare that your love stands firm forever,
that you established your faithfulness in heaven itself.

PSALM 89:1-2 NIV

Father's Day

I will remember the deeds of the LORD;
yes, I will remember your miracles of long ago.

PSALM 77:11 NIV

*F*or those of us who've been fathers for many years, Father's Day is a time for memories. We'll sit at our Father's Day dinner and someone will say, "Do you remember when . . . ?" It's a time when our children tell us what they remember best about their childhood.

It's a time when we tell our children funny stories about their growing-up years. Our children thank us, and we thank God for our children.

The life of faith is also a time of memories. Of remembering and telling each other what God has done for us. Remembering the deeds of the Lord naturally leads us to thanking God for all we have—especially these children, now grown, making memories and stories with their own children. We remember God's wonders of old—and are grateful.

*T*oday we can remember what God has done
for us—and we are thankful.

I will think about each
one of your mighty deeds.
PSALM 77:12 CEV

—⫘—

Children are a gift from the LORD;
they are a reward from him.
PSALM 127:3 NLT

God's Purpose for Us

We are your people, the sheep of your flock.
We will thank you always;
forever and ever we will praise you.

PSALM 79:13 NCV

—⁂—

God's ways are mysterious, but we know something about His purpose for us in this world. We know God loves us. Because God loves us, God wants us to make sure that the generations who come after us love God, praise God, and walk uprightly and in honor on the Earth.

That's where we come in. We are part of God's divine purpose to make sure that generation follows generation to give God thanks and praise. The most important part of fatherhood is to train and teach and raise our children to love God, to give God thanks and praise, and to grow into honorable adulthood, respecting others and doing good for those less fortunate. It's a powerful purpose. Being a father is a holy calling from God. We are both proud and humbled to carry out God's purpose.

—⁂—

We are fathers. Today we carry out God's purpose for us.

GOD is great, and worth a thousand Hallelujahs.
His terrible beauty makes the gods look cheap;
Pagan gods are mere tatters and rags.
GOD made the heavens—
Royal splendor radiates from him,
A powerful beauty sets him apart.
PSALM 96:3-4 THE MESSAGE

In order that the succeeding generation might know,
that the children still to be born might arise and recount it to their sons,
so as to put their confidence in God and not to forget God's works,
but to keep His commandments.
PSALM 78:6-7 MLB

A Father's Place

Even the sparrow has found a home,
and the swallow a nest for herself,
where she may have her young—
a place near your altar,
O LORD Almighty, my King and my God.

PSALM 84:3 NIV

———

*M*aybe it's because we are fathers that we care about our homes so much. We work hard to pay the mortgage, to keep our

homes in good repair, and to make our homes comfortable places for our families. We keep a garage full of tools to work on the house; we install appliances to help our wives keep our homes clean; some of us put in long hours in the garden to add to the value of our homes. There is truly no place like home.

So we spend a lot of time—and money—making sure our homes are the best places they can be.

Home is also a sanctuary. It is where we dwell with God every day. It may not be a very quiet place; it may be filled with children and pets and all. Even so, it is a place of peace, a place of wholeness—a place where we and our families can retreat from a fragmented and demanding world to find God.

———

*W*e are fathers, keepers of God's sanctuary, our homes.

How blessed are those
who dwell in Your house!
They are ever praising You.
PSALM 84:4 NASB

~m~

Because you have made the LORD, who is my refuge,
Even the Most High, your dwelling place,
No evil shall befall you,
Nor shall any plague come near your dwelling.
PSALM 91:9-10 NKJV

The Power of Self-Control

*The LORD God is a sun and shield;
the LORD bestows favor and honor;
no good thing does he withhold
from those whose walk is blameless.*

PSALM 84:11 NIV

——ᴍ——

*R*aising children usually means exercising some self-control over our lifestyles. Any couple can remember what it was like before the children started arriving. Vacationing at grown-up destinations instead of theme parks, driving a sporty two-door instead of a minivan, or going out to eat and sitting down in a restaurant with cloth napkins instead of eating fast food at a counter with a happy toy.

Self-control for the sake of our children is more than a lifestyle choice. It is making sure that we live a life that is pleasing to God. Such self-control is not hard—for God gives good things to those who walk uprightly. The benefit to our children is immense—they learn to live like Dad, who is generous, grateful, and full of love for God and His ways.

——ᴍ——

*T*he power of self-control is the love of God. He gives all good things to those who live life with honor and integrity.

Let thy work appear unto thy servants, and thy glory unto their children. And let the beauty of the LORD our God be upon us: and establish thou the work of our hands upon us; yea, the work of our hands establish thou it.

PSALM 90:16-17 KJV

—ɯ—

Create in me a clean heart, O God.
Renew a right spirit within me.

PSALM 51:10 NLT

Compassionate Fatherhood

Make glad the soul of Your servant,
For to You, O LORD, I lift up my soul.
For You, LORD, are good, and ready to forgive,
And abundant in lovingkindness to all who call upon You.

PSALM 86:4-5 NASB

We are compassionate by nature. One of the things we fathers do is cheer up a child who has had a bad day or is frightened or otherwise sad. We wipe away tears and try to divert their attention by helping them to do something fun—maybe a one-on-one basketball game in the backyard or a bike ride around the block or building a fort under the dining table.

Our God is compassionate too. Whenever we've had a bad day, we can go to God and ask Him to make our hearts glad again. We know that God is loving and good and forgiving—and God wants us to be happy. When we come to God like a child who needs cheering up, God will have compassion on us—His goodness and His love will make us glad.

God will gladden our souls and restore us to happiness again.

Mercy and truth have met together;
Righteousness and peace have kissed.
Truth shall spring out of the earth,
And righteousness shall look down from heaven.
PSALM 85:10-11 NKJV

—⁓—

My lips will praise you
because your mercy is better than life itself.
PSALM 63:3 GOD'S WORD

Gratitude—A Way of Life

I will praise You, O LORD my God, with all my heart,
And I will glorify Your name forevermore.

PSALM 86:12 NKJV

*W*e teach our children to say "please" and "thank you." In a small way it's a way of life, because saying "please" and "thank you" is more than just being polite—it's what makes us civilized. Saying "please" and "thank you" puts a little oil on the cogs and gears that make day-to-day social life possible. It helps us all to get along together.

Saying "thank You" to God is a way of life. In fact, a life lived in gratitude to God is a life lived in faith. Saying "thank You" to God—for His blessings, for watching over our children and us, and for His love, mercy, and grace—keeps our relationship with God growing. It's more than just being polite. Being grateful to God keeps us from taking God and His work in our lives for granted. Saying "Thank You, God" tells God we want Him in our lives.

*W*e give thanks to God today with our whole hearts.

It is good to give thanks
to the LORD,
to sing praises to your name,
O Most High;
to declare your steadfast love
in the morning,
and your
faithfulness by night.
PSALM 92:1-2 NRSV

They eat the rich food
in your house,
And you let them drink
from your river of pleasure.
You are the giver of life.
Your light lets us enjoy life.
PSALM 36:8-9 NCV

Promise Keeping

*E*very father knows how important promises are to children. When children make promises to each other, their promises are sealed with childhood vows to keep them, including chants to "stick a needle in my eye" or spit and handshakes. A child's world stands or falls depending on how well promises are kept. A broken promise

brings big screams of "but he promised!"

Fathers are promise keepers. We promise God to keep His words—to love and respect one another, to show mercy and forgiveness, to be men of faith. We promise our children to be the best fathers we can be, to love them and take care of them and raise them well. Our children watch us keeping our promise to God, and they grow up to be promise keepers too. They become people of faith, who love and respect one another, and promise to keep God's words.

*W*e will tell of God's faithfulness and promise to keep God's words.

You are my inheritance, O LORD.
I promised to hold on to your words.
PSALM 119:57 GOD'S WORD

—m—

Your word is a lamp for my feet
and a light for my path.
PSALM 119:105 NLT

Guardian Angels

He will command his angels concerning you
to guard you in all your ways.

PSALM 91:11 NRSV

—⟫⟪—

 *W*hat father hasn't waved good-bye to his children and said a silent prayer that God would send guardian angels to watch over them? When our children leave us, even for a little while, we pray for God's angels to defend and protect them. Our children's angels hover over them, go with them, and bring them safely home.

Fathers have guardian angels too. Because our work is important to God, He sends His angels to guard us in all our ways. We know that when we've had a particularly tough day at work or we need extra energy to help the kids do their homework, our guardian angel hovers over us, telling us God loves us. So the next time we stand at the front door waving good-bye, we know our own guardian angel watches over us and waits with us until our children return safely home.

—⟫⟪—

*T*oday God sends His guardian angels
to take care of our children and us.

Because he has set his love upon Me, therefore I will deliver him;
I will set him on high, because he has known My name.
He shall call upon Me, and I will answer him;
I will be with him in trouble;
I will deliver him and honor him.
With long life I will satisfy him,
And show him My salvation.

PSALM 91:14-16 NKJV

The angel of the LORD encamps around those who fear him,
and he delivers them.

PSALM 34:7 NIV

Fathers Are Optimists

*You, O Lᴏʀᴅ, have made me glad by what You have done,
I will sing for joy at the works of Your hands.*

Psᴀʟᴍ 92:4 ɴᴀsʙ

———ɯ———

A father is a natural optimist. A father looks at his child and sometimes thinks, *Maybe he's a future president of the United States, or maybe she'll be a nuclear physicist, or maybe she'll follow in her mother's footsteps.* Our dreams for our children make us optimists. That optimism helps give us the energy and foresight we need to make sure that our children's future is bright. We are full of pride and hope.

We are made glad by the works of God's hands, our children. As we behold God's work, we see a promise. Our hope is so great that we feel as though our souls could burst with pride. Being filled with hope and promise such as this almost makes us want to sing.

———ɯ———

*W*e've only to look in our children's eyes to see that today is filled with hope and promise.

Blessed are all who fear the LORD,
who walk in his ways.
PSALM 128:1 NIV

—⁓—

Our LORD and our God,
you give these blessings
to all who worship you.
PSALM 144:15 CEV

The Beauty of Worship

*O come, let us worship and bow down: let us kneel before the L*ORD *our maker. For he is our God; and we are the people of his pasture, and the sheep of his hand.*

PSALM 95:6-7 KJV

—⬯—

*F*athers are lots of good things—we're caring, we're good providers, we're optimistic, we're devoted to our children. There's one thing we're not—we're not in control. We're especially not in control of our children. What a great thing that is. Only God is in control of our lives and the lives of our children. God, our Maker, holds all of us in the palm of His hand. It is God, and God alone, who works for good in our lives.

When we worship God, we acknowledge that we are not in control and that we have faith and trust that God is in control of our world. Freedom is giving up trying to be in charge when we don't have to be. Freedom is giving God the reins and letting God do His work. When we worship God, we give up control and are free to be good fathers and to take care of our children.

—⬯—

*W*e are not the shepherds. We are the sheep of God's hand.

I bow before your holy Temple as I worship.
I will give thanks to your name
for your unfailing love and faithfulness,
because your promises are backed
by all the honor of your name.
When I pray, you answer me;
you encourage me by giving me the strength I need.

PSALM 138:2-3 NLT

—⁂—

Give unto the LORD the glory due unto his name;
worship the LORD in the beauty of holiness.

PSALM 29:2 KJV

The Creativity of Fatherhood

Sing to the LORD a new song;
sing to the LORD, all the earth.
Sing to the LORD, praise his name;
proclaim his salvation day after day.

PSALM 96:1-2 NIV

—ᴍ—

*F*athers are creative people. We use our creativity to entertain our children on a rainy day—from finger painting to modeling

clay. We spend hours in the garage teaching the kids how to build a birdhouse; we make countless videotapes and photographs of our children growing up—all because we love our children. Fatherhood is one big creative project.

In God's hands, fathers are instruments of God's creativity. We are like musical instruments played by a fine musician who plays songs that are fresh and new and have never been heard before. Children are like new songs—no two, not even twins, are exactly alike. Each child is a new, distinct, irreplaceable person. Each child is a new song that God sings.

—ᴍ—

*S*ing to the Lord a new song,
for we are instruments in His hands.

You alone created my inner being.
You knitted me together inside my mother.
I will give thanks to you
because I have been so amazingly
and miraculously made.
Your works are miraculous,
and my soul is fully aware of this.
PSALM 139:13-14 GOD'S WORD

Families Tell God's Glory

Ascribe to the LORD, O families of the peoples,
Ascribe to the Lord glory and strength.

PSALM 96:7 NASB

*O*ur families are our crown and glory. Not only do we love them, but we are also proud of who they are and what they do in the world. Even the family pet is a special source of pride. Our families tell the world a lot about us as fathers—they make us look good.

Families also tell the world a lot about God. A family bound together by the love and grace of God tells the world that God is loving and merciful. A family whose members love and respect one another because of God tells the world that God is strong and good. Not only are our families our own crown and glory, they are the glory of God. Families are God's pride and joy. Through families, God tells the world that He is at work in the world.

*O*ur families glorify God; they are jewels in God's crown.

Bless the LORD, O house of Israel!
Bless the LORD, O house of Aaron!
Bless the LORD, O house of Levi!
You who fear the LORD, bless the LORD!
PSALM 135:19-20 NKJV

A Quiet Morning with God

Light dawns for the righteous,
and joy for the upright in heart.

PSALM 97:11 NRSV

—⟋ℳ⟍—

Sometimes we awake early in the morning well before the alarm goes off. The house is so quiet. Wide awake, we're faced with a choice—we can toss and turn and fret when sleep won't come, or we can get up and do something useful.

Grab a light blanket and a Bible and head for the couch. There in the predawn quiet we can do something truly useful— we can spend a quiet morning with God. We can open the Bible anywhere and read until a verse touches us. We can reread favorite passages and pray. Sometimes, even at three A.M., our hearts may be full of joy—we can talk quietly to God, who is the Source of all joy. When sleep finally begins to return, we can thank God for being His child and head back to bed.

—⟋ℳ⟍—

*J*oy comes in the morning for God's children.

I could say, "The darkness will hide me.
Let the light around me turn into night."
But even the darkness is not dark to you.
The night is as light as the day.
Darkness and light are the same to you.
PSALM 139:11-12 NCV

Awake, my glory!
Awake, lute and harp!
I will awaken the dawn.
PSALM 57:8 NKJV

We Know Who We Are

O Lord, You have searched me and known me.

PSALM 139:1 NKJV

———

*W*hat father hasn't looked at his sleeping child at some time and felt awed and humbled? During such moments we know that this is what life is really all about. We want nothing more than to be the father of this amazing gift, our child.

Humility is a spiritual gift. It doesn't mean we walk around putting ourselves down or thinking badly of ourselves. Instead, true humility is knowing who we really are—and thanking God for who we are in this life. Our friends or the people at work may think they know us. We know who we really are underneath all those other roles—we are fathers, chosen by God to bring our children into this world and raise them to love and honor God. Fatherhood is a calling that inspires awe—and true humility—in us. We can rejoice and thank God that we know who we are.

———

*F*atherhood is a humble, valuable gift of God.

As a father has compassion on his children,
so the LORD has compassion on those who fear him;
for he knows how we are formed,
he remembers that we are dust.
PSALM 103:13-14 NIV

Fathers Model Integrity

I will sing of lovingkindness and justice,
To You, O LORD, I will sing praises.

PSALM 101:1-2 NASB

———

When we're dealing with a person of integrity, we know that "what you see is what you get." A person of integrity does what he says he's going to do. A person of integrity has no hidden agendas. A person of integrity lives his beliefs. A person of integrity inspires

trust and loyalty in others. A person of integrity is just a good person.

All fathers want their children to grow up into people of integrity. We model integrity for our children when our behavior is consistent with our faith—when we keep our promises, when we have mercy on those less fortunate, and when we generously share our love of God. Fathers who model integrity "walk the talk." Our children are watching our every move, eager to copy what we do and say. Over the years they grow into strong adults who love God and walk with integrity of heart.

———

With the love of God and the practice of our faith let us model integrity for our children.

May the LORD bless you from Zion
All the days of your life;
May you see the prosperity of Jerusalem,
And may you live to see your children's children.

PSALM 128:5-6 NIV

Our Children's Heritage

The children of Your servants will continue,
And their descendants will be established before You.

PSALM 102:28 NKJV

—ᴍ—

*W*hen a father becomes a grandfather, it's as though all of our dreams have finally come true. It's a different kind of miracle from fatherhood. To hold our grandchildren in our arms is to hold a

little bit of the future that we will never see. When we're with our grandchildren, we feel ourselves to be a link in an incredibly long family chain. We rejoice and give thanks that God has let us see our children's children.

Our faith is for generations. The trust and belief we have in God are gifts to future generations, who will learn from us the joy of loving God. As grandfathers, we can show our grandchildren God's way. It is our grandchildren who will carry our faith deep into the future for generations to come. In a very real sense, a grandfather's faith is forever.

—ᴍ—

*O*ur children's heritage—our grandchildren—
is the future in God's hands.

You want me to be
completely truthful.
so teach me wisdom.
PSALM 51:6 NCV

Some trust in chariots, and
some in horses: but we will
remember the name of the
LORD our God.
PSALM 20:7 KJV

The Benefits of Believing

Bless the LORD, O my soul;
and all that is within me,
bless his holy name.
Bless the LORD, O my soul,
and forget not all his benefits.

PSALM 103:1-2 NRSV

———

*T*hough they may be easy to forget during a particularly hectic day, there are many benefits to fatherhood. We get to watch our children grow up. We get to play with them as well as provide for them. We get to take pleasure in the love of our children when they are little. When they are grown, we get to enjoy them as adults.

There are many benefits to believing in God too. We get to experience God's mercy and grace when we make mistakes. We get to feel God's love when we look in on our napping children. We get to thank God for giving us all that we need to live and survive. We get to worship God, the Creator of our children—and our children's children. We wouldn't trade fatherhood or our life of faith for anything in the world.

———

*W*e will remember all the benefits of believing in God today.

Blessed be the LORD,
Who daily loads us with benefits,
The God of our salvation!
PSALM 68:19 NKJV

Fathers and Other Living Things

O Lord, how manifold are Your works!
In wisdom You have made them all.
The earth is full of Your possessions—
This great and wide sea,
In which are innumerable teeming things,
Living things both small and great.

Psalm 104:24-25 nkjv

———

Cats. Dogs. Hamsters. Several frogs over a period of time. A turtle. Goldfish. Maybe a bunny rabbit. Kids and animals go together. Eventually, we end up taking care of pets as well as children. The innocence and helplessness of animals and children speak to us, and so we take care of both.

There's something about being fathers that forms a special connection between all of God's creatures and us. We know God cares for the animals He makes. The connection is creation. Our instinct to care for our children—and even their pets—is rooted in God the Creator. We enjoy all God's creatures, great and small.

———

God loves all the children and animals. So do we.

Ships sail on it,
and Leviathan, which you made, plays in it.
All of them look to you to give them their food at the right time.
You give it to them, and they gather it up.
You open your hand, and they are filled with blessings.

PSALM 104:26-28 GOD'S WORD

Fathers Don't Give Up

Seek the L<small>ORD</small>, and his strength: seek his face evermore.
Remember his marvellous works that he hath done;
his wonders, and the judgments of his mouth;
O ye seed of Abraham his servant, ye children of Jacob his chosen.

P<small>SALM</small> 105:4-6 KJV

*F*athers persevere. It's not in our nature to give up when the going gets tough. Sure, we've got a lot on our plates—we're full-time fathers in addition to full-time wage-earners. We manage. We

cope. Most of the time, we juggle our lives very well—we have to because the well-being of our children is at stake.

Fathers persevere in another way too. We are always seeking God and His strength. There's so much to do that we can't afford not to do. We know that when we are in touch with God He will give us all we need to be good fathers. We know that when we search for God we find that God is walking right beside us.

*T*oday we can persevere because we have found God.

As the eyes of slaves look to the hand of their master,
as the eyes of a maid look to the hand of her mistress,
so our eyes look to the LORD our God,
till he shows us his mercy.
PSALM 123:2 NIV

The LORD is my strength,
my shield from every danger.
I trust in him with all my heart.
He helps me, and my heart is filled with joy.
I burst out in songs of thanksgiving.
PSALM 28:7 NLT

Love Is Forever

Great is your love, higher than the heavens;
your faithfulness reaches to the skies.

PSALM 108:4 NIV

A father's love is limitless. Our love for our children doesn't stop when they grow up. Instead our love deepens and grows with them. When our children have children of their own, even more love is born in our hearts. A father's love is so big it may even expand beyond our own families to include friends and neighbors. When we became fathers, God gave us big hearts.

God's love is forever. God loves us and our children and all that is in our world. God's love is not limited by time. God gives us His love all our days—and well beyond, in heaven. There is no place we can go that God's love can't find us. There is nothing we can do to stop God from loving us. Touched by God's eternal love as we are, we know that our hearts will always be faithful.

*O*ur love is limitless because God loves us forever.

I'm ready, God, so ready,
ready from head to toe.
Ready to sing,
ready to raise a God-song:
"Wake, soul! Wake, lute!
Wake up, you sleepyhead sun!"
PSALM 108:1-3 THE MESSAGE

He ransoms me from death
and surrounds me with love and tender mercies.
PSALM 103:4 NLT

A Father's Comfort

It was you who took me from the womb;
you kept me safe on my mother's breast.
On you I was cast from my birth,
and since my mother bore me you have been my God.

Psalm 22:9-10 NRSV

—⁓—

$\mathcal{A}$ father's life is adventure. The adventure begins when our children come into our life. Along the way we love them. We help nurse them when they are sick. We help them with their schoolwork. We coach them through Little League, ballet, soccer, or violin lessons. We get them to do their chores and nag them about finishing everything on their plates. Through all the adventures that fatherhood brings, God travels with us and watches over us and comforts us.

Suddenly our children graduate, marry, and have children of their own. Our love swells with pride. We know they have begun a great adventure. Even though we may even shed a few tears of joy and pride as our children set off on their journeys, we know that God goes with them—to love them as God has loved them from birth. Our heart is comforted.

—⁓—

$\mathcal{A}$t the beginning of all great adventures in life, we can take comfort in how our God loves us with a father's love.

When I am afraid, I put my trust in you.
O God, I praise your word.
I trust in God, so why should I be afraid?
What can mere mortals do to me?

PSALM 56:3-4 NLT

The Apple of God's Eye

Guard me as the apple of the eye;
hide me in the shadow of your wings.

PSALM 17:8 NRSV

———

*F*atherhood is about giving. We give our time and love in abundance to raise our children well. We give because our children are the apples of our eyes. How could we possibly give anything less?

To keep giving every day, fathers need lots of strength. The

strength that can keep us going is the knowledge of how much God loves us. God loves each one of us deeply and faithfully because each of us is the apple of God's eye, protected under the shadow of God's wing. We are so dear to God. God is so much in love with us that He loves us as His children. God gives us what we need every day so we can give even more to our children, the apples of our eyes. Under the shadow of God's wing, we draw strength from which we give.

———

*Y*ou are a father—the apple of God's eye, kept safe under the shadow of God's wing.

As the mountains surround Jerusalem,
So the LORD surrounds his people
Both now and forevermore.
PSALM 125:2 NIV

Time for God

As a deer longs for flowing streams,
so my soul longs for you, O God.
My soul thirsts for God,
for the living God.

PSALM 42:1-2 NRSV

—⅏—

*F*athers are very busy people. There are Little League games to attend, scraped knees to bandage, chores to supervise, and homework to oversee. A lot is crammed into a father's day—usually at the beginning and the end of a hectic day at work.

To keep going at such a fast clip, we need to replenish our own thirsty souls. We need time with God, even if it's only a stolen moment or two on the run. Simply thinking about God, who loves us deeply, can quench our thirst for a while. Or thanking God for the love of children and home  can keep us going when we're dashing off to the next meeting. If a father's faith is to stay strong, a drink from God's fountain can sustain us in all we do.

—⅏—

*T*oday may be busy, and yet we can take a moment to drink from God's flowing streams.

The LORD shows his true love every day.
At night I have a song,
and I pray to my living God.
PSALM 42:8 NCV

—m—

Deal bountifully with Your servant,
That I may live and keep Your word.
Open my eyes, that I may behold
Wonderful things from Your law.
PSALM 119:17-18 NASB

If you have enjoyed this book, you will also enjoy other gift books available from your local bookstore.

GIFTS FROM MY GARDEN
GIFTS FROM MY FRONT PORCH
DAILY BLESSINGS FOR MY HUSBAND
DAILY BLESSINGS FOR MY WIFE
DAILY BLESSINGS FOR MY SECRET PAL
LETTERS FROM GOD
LETTERS FROM GOD FOR TEENS
LIGHTHOUSE PSALMS
FRIENDSHIP PSALMS
GARDEN PSALMS
LOVE PSALMS
PSALMS FOR MOTHERS
PSALMS FOR WOMEN

*If this book has impacted your life,
we would like to hear from you.*

Please contact us at:

Honor Books
Department E
P. O. Box 55388
Tulsa, Oklahoma 74155

Or by e-mail at:
info@honorbooks.com